T0142527

for women only

Discussion Guide

shaunti feldhahn

with Lisa A. Rice

Multnomah Books

FOR WOMEN ONLY DISCUSSION GUIDE

Published in association with the literary agency of
Calvin Edwards, 1220 Austin Glen Drive, Atlanta, GA 30338
© 2005 by Veritas Enterprises, Inc.
International Standard Book Number: 978-1-59052-768-9

Cover photo by PixelWorks Studios, www.shootpw.com
Interior design and typeset by Katherine Lloyd, The DESK

Scripture quotations are from:
Holy Bible, New Living Translation
© 1996. Used by permission of Tyndale House Publishers, Inc.
All rights reserved.

Published in the United States by Multnomah, an imprint of the Crown
Publishing Group, a division of Penguin Random House LLC, New York.

MULTNOMAH® and its mountain colophon are registered trademarks
of Penguin Random House LLC.

146086900

Contents

Chapter 1

LIGHTBULB ON!

How I Woke Up to What I Didn't Know About Men

Since *For Women Only* came out, I have been so grateful to hear from women all over the country who tell me, "My eyes have been opened—and I can't believe I didn't know some of these things before!" That excitement is inevitably followed by: "So, um, how do I apply this to *my* life?"

This discussion guide will help you do just that. It is designed to be used in two different ways: as a catalyst for conversations among women in small or large groups, in book clubs or coffee klatches, or as a helpful roadmap for a good one-on-one dialogue with the man in your life.

As I have spoken around the country, I have run across many women doing *For Women Only* discussion groups. I'm very grateful for those who have been willing to share their ideas, many of which have been incorporated in these pages. Near the end of this guide we also share the suggestions of two study groups who have used this discussion guide itself since it first came out.

Because of the wonderful variety and diversity I've encountered among different groups, this guide is intended to be very flexible. But for consistency and ease of use, each chapter in the guide follows the same format and each corresponds to a chapter subject in the book:

- Chapter 2: Respect
- Chapter 3: Insecurity
- Chapter 4: The Provider Burden
- Chapter 5: Sex
- Chapter 6: Visual
- Chapter 7: Romance
- Chapter 8: Appearance
- Chapter 9: "How much I love her"

Each chapter has the same layout. The first few pages are for group discussion. The last two pages contain space for notes and a section called "Bringing It Home" that's just for one-on-one discussion with your man.

The order is consistent in every chapter, with such features as:

- A Recap of the chapter
- Key Questions for discussion
- A true Life Story case study with follow-up questions
- A Guy Perspective and Gal Response
- A *For Women Only* (FWO) Feedback section, which includes e-mails and personal stories from women (and sometimes from their husbands!) who have read *For Women Only* and benefited from that particular subject, along with a question to consider.

- A Weekly Challenge—A question that requires self-examination and a challenge to actually *apply* what you are learning about your man.
- Bringing It Home: Discussing It with Your Man— sample questions that might help.
- A Quote to Remember
- Suggested further reading

The guide is designed to be completely flexible as far as number of weeks that you meet, and mixing and matching the elements to suit your group. For example, some groups may opt to cover one subject per session, going through each of the elements in detail, while others may want to combine chapters and only tackle the Key Questions of each. Some groups may want to pick only one Key Question each week and instead focus on the mini-case studies and Weekly Challenges. Pick and choose whichever works for you.

I hope this guide will be interesting and helpful for all female audiences, whether married, dating, or single. As you leaf through this, you'll find that I use the words "guy," "man," and "husband" somewhat interchangeably. (The only exception is when discussing sex, since I agree with the biblical principle of reserving physical intimacy for marriage.) I'm primarily focusing on helping you apply these truths to your romantic relationship, but many of the issues affect how you relate to other important men in your life as well, such as perhaps your son or your boss. Feel free to branch out into those subjects where warranted.

As you read and discuss, please remember that *For Women Only* is not an equal treatment of male-female differences, nor does this guide delve much into what guys need to understand about us. Although we women obviously have needs too, for right now, this is solely about helping us understand the inner lives of men and how we relate to them. Ultimately, it is not supposed to help us "change our guy"—these revelations are supposed to change and improve us!

Many of us—including me—have found that the data in *For Women Only* sometimes goes against decades of assumptions about men, and you will likely feel the gamut of emotions as various facts and truths hit you. Please be careful about unloading these emotions on your man. When you do discuss these things with him, remember that it is all too easy for a man to feel insecure and "attacked," and he will respond much better if he feels that you are respecting him—which, as we learn in Chapter 2, is his highest need anyway.

The following chart outlines the seven major findings from the *For Women Only* research. The column on the left, "our surface understanding" is what we women generally know from a distance about men, whereas the column on the right, "What That Means in Practice," is a focused—and often surprising—finding about how that plays out in everyday life.

The Seven Revelations

Our Surface Understanding (What we already tend to think)	What That Means in Practice
1. Men need respect.	Men would rather feel alone and unloved than inadequate and disrespected.
2. Men are insecure.	Despite their "in control" exteriors, men often feel like impostors and are insecure that their inadequacies will be discovered.
3. Men are providers.	Even if you personally made enough income to support the family's lifestyle, it would make no difference to the mental burden he feels to provide.
4. Men want more sex.	Your sexual desire for your husband profoundly affects his sense of well-being and confidence in all areas of life.
5. Men are visual.	Even happily married men struggle with being pulled toward live and recollected images of other women.
6. Men are unromantic clods.	Actually, most men enjoy romance (sometimes in different ways) and want to be romantic—but hesitate because they doubt they can succeed.
7. Men care about appearance.	You don't need to be a size 3, but your man does need to see you making the effort to take care of yourself—and he will take on significant cost or inconvenience in order to support you.

My best to you in your journey!

Shaunti

P.S. If your group has an introductory week, here's your first Weekly Challenge question:

Weekly Challenge: This week, identify which of the seven revelations on the chart you are already implementing best, and which one is the most likely to require changes in your life.

Chapter 2

YOUR LOVE
IS *NOT* ENOUGH

Why Your Respect Means More to Him than Even Your Affection

<u>Weekly Challenge Report:</u> In which of the seven areas are you already excelling at supporting your man? Which area needs the most work?

The Recap

Your respect means more to your man than even your affection. Three-quarters of men would rather feel alone and unloved than inadequate and disrespected. Men need to be respected—in public and in private—in the areas of their judgment, abilities, communication, and assumptions. It's not about male pride; it's about feelings of inadequacy. And his highest need is feeling that you trust him, regardless. You as a woman can help by assuming the best and choosing to demonstrate respect to him unconditionally, just as you want him to love you unconditionally.

"Just as our men can choose to demonstrate love toward us even if they don't feel it at the moment, we can and should choose to demonstrate respect." —Shaunti, FWO, p. 27

"'The only time a guy's guard is completely down is with the woman he loves. So she can pierce his heart like no one else.'" —Man Quote, FWO, p. 44

Key Questions

1. What challenged you most in this chapter?
2. Relate an example of a time you conveyed disrespect to your man—even if you didn't mean to. Also, give an example of when you "got it right."
3. Does your man tell you when he feels disrespected? Or does he show it in another way? What is his way of responding to disrespect or a lack of trust?
4. How do you talk about your husband to your family? To your friends? To his friends?
5. Consider the marriage advice of the apostle Paul: "So again I say, each man must love his wife as he loves himself, and the wife must respect her husband" (Ephesians 5:33). What is the connection between a husband loving his wife and a wife respecting her husband?

Life Story

Nicole and Blake were on a beach vacation with their family and signed up for a shark-watching tour. However, Blake didn't feel their youngest child—three-year-old Josh—was mature enough to come along. Nicole was angry. She didn't want to deprive any of her children of such a memorable adventure, and she didn't want to leave Josh behind to spend a boring day with a babysitter. The couple had a major argument, with Nicole telling Blake, "I can respect you when you're doing well and drawing the children into life, but not when you're making your decisions out of fear." Blake answered, "So you've chosen to trust me, what, about half the time?"

Case Study Questions

1. What did Nicole do wrong, if anything?
2. Put yourself in Blake's shoes for a moment. What would you feel as the recipient of Nicole's "I can respect you when…" comment?
3. Stay in Blake's shoes. What might be some of the reasons he didn't want Josh to come?
4. Does Blake deserve Nicole's respect and adherence to his plans even in cases where she strongly disagrees?

5. How were the words "respect" and "trust" interchangeable in the above scenario? Do you think these terms are synonymous to your man?

6. What would have been the ideal response from Nicole?

Guy Perspective: "I met the new president of a large business last week, and after being with him for a day, I concluded that what makes him most successful is his ability to listen to and respect the feelings of other men and make them feel that they are important—whether it's the janitor or VP. Every guy will kill himself to work for this man."

Gal Response: Are you surprised that men will "kill themselves" to work in an environment where they're respected? Why or why not?

For Women Only (FWO) **Female Feedback (via e-mail):** "I am a pastor's wife and have been married for almost seventeen years, and while I felt like I knew things about men and the differences (Mars/Venus thing)—after reading your book I felt like I had *the biggest aha moment* of our entire relationship. The whole issue of their needing respect versus feeling alone/unloved made so much sense. I have struggled so much with wanting to do things "my way"... feeling that my husband's input was trying too much to control or be "right." Now I realize that I show my respect for him by listening and implementing his suggestions.

Housecleaning is a *huge* one for us. My husband would love to come home Friday night with everything on the inside done for the week. He has even told me that he's *fine* if I take off and go play all day Saturday; he'd just love to have the house cleaned by Friday night so he has the weekend in a peaceful home. But have I ever done it? Up to two weeks ago, no. Why? I can't even explain it except that I am a procrastinator and do it all on Saturday—even though I know it creates hassle when he most needs rest. But now I realize that not only am I providing a place of rest for him, but because he has asked...I am respecting him."

Consider: Can you relate? Is there something your man has asked you to do—or not do—and you find yourself making excuses? Is it demeaning to you as a woman to implement suggestions (or requests) like this one?

Weekly Challenge: 1) Observe the men in your life—including the men you work with—and try to spot three situations where they might be feeling disrespected. 2) Find three concrete ways to show genuine respect to your guy.

BRINGING IT HOME:
DISCUSSING IT WITH YOUR MAN

Dear Hubby...

- What are *your* answers to the survey questions in this chapter?

- What in my actions or words most makes you feel respected? Disrespected?

- When you did this _____, it made me feel like you were doing/saying this: _____. But now I realize maybe you were doing/saying this: _____; is that correct?
Since examples may help me "see" this better:

- Can you give me an example of a time that I really made you feel trusted?

- Can you give me an example of a time when you felt that I didn't trust or respect you?

- Confidentially, which other couples that we know have respectful behavior patterns and which do not?

- How do you feel our parents related to each other in this area of respect? How can our marriage improve upon their patterns?

A Quote to Remember:

"There is no respect for others without humility in one's self."
—Henri Frederic Amiel

Suggested further reading:

Love and Respect by Emerson Eggerichs

The **BIG** Idea

The one main idea I'm taking away from this week's discussion is:

_____

_____

_____

_____

_____

_____

_____

_____

_____

_____

_____

_____

_____

_____

Chapter 3

THE PERFORMANCE
OF A LIFETIME

Why Your Mr. Smooth Looks So Impressive but Feels Like an Impostor

Weekly Challenge Report: Did you spot "disrespect" examples? What ways did you find to show genuine respect to your man?

The Recap

Despite their in-control exterior, men often feel like impostors and are insecure that their inadequacies will be discovered. Men believe they're being watched and judged constantly, and two-thirds admit to feigning competency despite feelings of inadequacy. Yet the conquering part of men loves the challenge. The key for women is constant affirmation and the creation of a "safety zone" at home.

"The male sense of performance anxiety doesn't, as one man put it, 'Just end when we walk through the front door.'" —Shaunti, FWO, p. 65

"Of the men I surveyed, only one man in four felt actively appreciated by his family." —Shaunti, FWO, p. 68

"It's about sending the man we love into the world every day, alive with the belief that he can slay dragons." —Shaunti, FWO, p. 74

Key Questions

1. What surprised you most about this chapter?

2. Give an example of when you unintentionally made your man feel *more* insecure, not less. Give an example of when you had an opportunity to affirm him, and counteract his secret insecurity.

3. How do you think women differ, if they do, in the areas of inadequacy, insecurity, and "the impostor syndrome"?

4. How do you feel when you perceive weakness or insecurity in your man?

5. What can you do to create an affirming, safe haven for the guy you love?

Life Story

Last summer Nicole and Blake were out with their new friends Sam and Gayle. At one point Blake suggested that the foursome go boating at a nearby lake. Knowing that her husband disliked boating and the motion sickness he usually felt, Gayle piped up, "Oh, we'd better not. Sam's not a strong swimmer, and he avoids boats like the plague." The others quickly made some alternative suggestions, but they could see that Sam was angry with his wife. Gayle loved her husband dearly and made frequent attempts to turn potentially embarrassing situations light and funny, but something obviously wasn't working.

Case Study Questions

1. What did Gayle do wrong, if anything, regarding Sam?

2. Put yourself in Sam's shoes. How does he view Gayle's attempts to be helpful?

3. What could she have done differently?

Guy Perspective: "The word *vulnerability* is a swearword to us guys. It means setting ourselves up to be exposed as less than we appear. We hate being vulnerable with other men because we're afraid the information might bite us down the road and our weaknesses and failings will be revealed to the world. A guy can make a million dollars, but if there's something he knows he's not good at, or if he feels 'less than' in an area, he's vulnerable to attack, and that's bad. It colors everything."

Gal Response: Do you think men have just as hard a time being vulnerable with wives or girlfriends as they do at work? Do you believe vulnerability is essential for healthy relationships in both men and women, and if so, how can you help your man feel like he can be vulnerable with you?

FWO Female Feedback: After reading the book, Tanya shared that she came from a family of divorce. She never fully understood why her parents divorced until one day when she found some very enlightening papers in an old desk drawer. Her father had written out the pros and cons of staying married. The "con" section far outweighed the "pro" section, and several of the "cons" were extremely eye opening. One of them read, "She acts like her mother, who always made me feel stupid." Another read, "She'll make me feel like I don't know what I'm doing with the children." Tanya reflected, through tears, on the truth of her father's feelings. Her mother had often criticized her father and made him feel that he didn't measure up. Though her mother would say she was just fine-tuning the marriage, obviously her father was absorbing only messages of inadequacy. Tanya vowed to forgive her mother and to take tangible steps to not repeat the negative cycle in her own marriage.

Consider: Do you see that such generational family patterns repeat themselves? If so, is it possible to break the cycle? How?

Weekly Challenge: 1) Observe the man in your life and try to spot at least three potential areas where he might feel like an impostor. 2) If you catch yourself stepping on your man's toes in this area, find a creative alternative to your usual response.

BRINGING IT HOME:
DISCUSSING IT WITH YOUR MAN

Dear Hubby...

- What are *your* answers to the survey questions in this chapter?

- Read the story on pp. 53–54 of *For Women Only*. Have you ever felt like Jean-Luc Picard? Do you ever feel that way at home? Elsewhere?

- How do I make you feel like you measure up at home— as a husband, father, provider, and lover?

- Can you give me an example of a time I got it right? Wrong?

- Do you consider our home a haven of unconditional acceptance? Is there anything I could change to make it more so?

- As I learn, will you help me to "get" this by *gently* pointing out when I do or say something that makes you feel pretty bad about yourself?

A Quote to Remember:

"You cannot consistently perform in a manner which is inconsistent with the way you see yourself." —Zig Ziglar

Suggested further reading:

Wild at Heart by John Eldredge

The **BIG** idea

The one main idea I'm taking away from this week's discussion is:

....

....

....

....

....

....

....

....

....

....

....

....

....

....

....

Chapter 4

THE LONELIEST BURDEN

How His Need to Provide Weighs Your Man Down, and Why He Likes it That Way

<u>Weekly Challenge Report:</u> Did you spot any potential impostor situations with your man last week? Did you find a creative alternative to your usual responses?

The Recap

Even if you alone earned enough income to provide for your family, it would make no difference to the mental burden your husband feels to provide. Being a provider is at the core of a man's identity. Men feel powerful when they provide, and providing is a way to express their love. Wives often get exasperated when husbands work late, which frustrates men because they think their long work hours (and the income that comes with it) are saying "I love you." Women can help by choosing not to nag, by contributing what they can to the family budget (if that is consistent with the family's shared career decisions), and by refusing to engage in unnecessary spending.

"Men feel powerful when they provide. And they want to be depended on." —Shaunti, FWO, p 79.

"'Why do you think I do work this much? It's because I care about you.'" —Man Quote, FWO, p. 81

"A man will internalize your disappointment as a personal failure to provide." —Shaunti, FWO, p. 89

Key Questions

1. What encouraged you most about this chapter?
2. What did you learn about men and their need to provide? How have you seen this played out in the relationships closest to you?
3. Give an example of a time when you may have added to your man's sense of "provider burden" or not appreciated the depth of it. Give an example of when you "got it right."
4. How do you respond when your man works long hours?
5. What can you do to alleviate the burden?

Life Story

Blake has his own business providing audio and video services for conventions. He loves his work, is good at it, and over the years, he and Nicole have gotten used to the industry's seasonal fluctuations. However, during one particularly tight year, Nicole's mother and a friend began regularly expressing their concern about Blake's ability to safely take the family into retirement years. Nicole, always very practical, began subtly asking him to find a "real" job with benefits and a 401(k). Blake asked her to be patient, not to rush into a major change, and to trust that God would lead them. Nicole replied that God helps those who help themselves. Increasingly, the couple argued about the subject. Nicole felt torn between her desire to support her hardworking husband and her desire to listen to the counsel of trusted others and nudge the family down a more practical financial path.

Case Study Questions

1. What did Nicole do right, and what did she do wrong in this story?

2. Put yourself in Blake's shoes. How do you think he is feeling about his ability to provide?

3. What might be some of the reasons that he didn't want to find another job? Would understanding those things help Nicole?
4. What should Nicole do differently, if anything?

Guy Perspective: "The burden to provide is so great that when it's eased for a while—even just a little—it feels fantastic. If it can't be lightened, the weight can break the back of the bearer. When the burden is shared, whether emotionally, tangibly (increasing dollars or decreasing lifestyle), or through encouragement, life feels so much lighter and easier. When a man is encouraged, supported, and appreciated—even if he's not Mr. Big Bucks—he feels better as a man."

Gal Response: How does it make you feel to know that your man feels this constant pressure? What can you do to help?

FWO Female Feedback: Last week Gina—a stay-at-home-mom—came up after a meeting and shared her story about the difficulty of this subject. She explained that, for several years, her husband, Jake, had asked her to live very modestly. He said he had been looking at their budget, and he wanted to make some changes that would hurt now and benefit them later. He asked Gina if there were some ways she could help—like not getting her hair highlighted, not getting the acrylic nails she loved so much, and holding off on decorating. She couldn't believe it. These were three of her major hot buttons, and she was miffed.

To make things worse, several of her friends were feeding her fury by saying things like, "He's not your master, Tina... You should have equal say in these repressive decisions... No woman should be expected to live this tightly... It's not reasonable... You don't have to take this, you know."

Gina decided to pray about it. And as she did, she really felt like she should honor Jake's requests, and trust that God still understood the desires of her heart. It was tough, and often she felt like the homely little wife, but she made the choice to trust him in this area of finances he felt so strongly about.

How did it turn out?

"Now, after about five years of living tightly like that," says Tina, "I'm here to tell you that God honored Jake's plan and my honoring of his strong opinion about this as our family's sole provider. I am now living in a totally paid-for house, our debt is gone, and I can get my hair and nails done any time I want. Best of all, my husband trusts me that I trust him with these decisions."

Consider: Have you and your man ever had similar issues? How might your response have differed from Gina's? What grade do you think she got on this test?

<u>Weekly Challenge:</u> Keep track of how many times you've shown appreciation for all your man does in the area of provision. What imaginative ways can you find to ease his "provider burden" and ease his mind a bit?

BRINGING IT HOME: DISCUSSING IT WITH YOUR MAN

Dear Hubby...

- What are *your* answers to the survey questions in this chapter?

- When you did this _____, it made me feel like you were doing/feeling this: _____. But now I realize maybe you were doing/feeling this: _____; is that correct?

- Give me an example of when you felt that I really understood the burden you feel to provide.

- Can you give me an example of when you felt that I didn't? How did that make you feel?

- Would it be easier for you if we reduced our lifestyle?

- How can I take some of the pressure off you?

Hint: One stay-at-home mom shared something she started doing to ensure her own financial peace, nip the worried nagging, and supplement her husband's income. She collected loose change in a specific container, and any time it got full she brought it to the grocery store and put it into the machine that converted it into cash. She opened a savings account at the bank inside the store and began depositing her extra dollars, getting highly motivated as she saw the balance climbing. Her husband was thrilled when she surprised him with her successful secret a year later.

A Quote to Remember:

"The harvest of old age is the recollection and abundance of blessing previously secured." —Cicero

"I'm living so far beyond my income that we may almost be said to be living apart." —e e cummings

Suggested further reading:

The Total Money Makeover by Dave Ramsey

The **BIG** Idea

The one main idea I'm taking away from this week's discussion is:

....

....

....

....

....

....

....

....

....

....

....

Chapter 5

SEX CHANGES EVERYTHING

Why Sex Unlocks a Man's Emotions (Guess Who Holds the Key?)

<u>Weekly Challenge Report:</u> How often did you show appreciation to your man for his provision? What ways did you find to ease or understand his "provider burden"?

The Recap

Your sexual desire for your husband profoundly affects his sense of well-being and confidence in all areas of his life. Men want to be wanted, and three-quarters would still feel empty if their wife wasn't both sexually engaged and sexually satisfied. If this area is lacking, a man feels a deep sense of personal rejection and even depression. It usually takes an overt decision for a woman to get tuned in, involved, passionate, creative, and committed to ensuring that her husband feels desired by her.

"At the most basic level, your man wants to be wanted."
—Shaunti, FWO, p. 93

"'Making love is a solace that goes very deep into the heart of a man.'" —Man Quote, FWO, p. 97

"'What happens in the bedroom really does affect how I feel the next day at the office.'" —Man Quote, FWO, p. 99

Key Questions

1. Were you surprised about the men's responses in this chapter, and the extreme *emotional* ramifications of sex—or the lack of it?

2. If the emotional importance is true, what message does it send a man when his wife *initiates* sex?

3. What are some obstacles that may get in the way of a woman being an involved, passionate partner in intimacy? How can those be addressed?

4. Consider this quote on pp. 96–97: "In making love, there is one other person in this world that you can be completely vulnerable with and be totally accepted and nonjudged. It is a solace that goes very deep into the heart of a man." If you are married, do you think your husband sees it that way? Does that change the way you view your husband's approaches?

Life Story

During their first year of marriage, Nicole and Blake enjoyed the physical intimacies of their new life together. During year two, however, Nicole took a community service position that she found both exhilarating and demanding. Despite coming home exhausted many evenings, she tried to make sure Blake knew she was always (well, nearly always) sexually available, even if sometimes she seemed to be "going through the motions." As the months passed, Nicole noticed that Blake began to seem somewhat withdrawn, even despondent. When she asked him about it, he said that things had changed. She used to be loving, available, adoring, and even inviting; now she was someone else, he said. Her work and community relationships seemed to have stolen her away. And their sex life just wasn't the same—some weeks the two were acting more like roommates than lovers. Blake's remarks confused Nicole. Yes, thinking back, she probably had been too tired to make love several times when he tried to initiate it, but she was doing everything she could to be a good wife. Didn't Blake understand that she was only one woman?

Case Study Questions

1. Make a list of the positive and negative messages Nicole was sending Blake.
2. Put yourself in Blake's shoes for a moment: Why was he becoming withdrawn and even despondent? What might the word *available* convey to him?
3. Is there a solution for this couple?
4. Could these complaints reveal some underlying issues beneath the surface, and if so, what might they be?

Guy Perspective: "If women knew how easy we are, they'd have it made. If a man gets regular, enthusiastic sex, she gets the world. It's really pretty simple."

Gal Response: If you think the above sentiment is true for most men, what's the holdup for most women? Is this *too* simple, and if so, what are the factors that complicate the deal?

FWO Female Feedback: "I cannot tell you how much your information regarding my responsibility in our sexual relationship has put the spark back into our 13 year marriage. I realized that our sex life had been so boring and mundane. I have to tell you that knowing how my husband's mind works has helped me to take care of myself physically and to take care of him sexually. Thank you for your hard work. I am a licensed professional counselor and will use your book with all of my female clients struggling in their marriage. Thank you, again."

Weekly Challenge:

For married women: This week, track what messages you may be sending your husband, either through your availability or lack of it. In what ways can you make progress in understanding and meeting the needs of his heart through sexual intimacy?

For single women: This week, observe the way the media portrays a man's view of sex. What message does it convey?

BRINGING IT HOME:
DISCUSSING IT WITH YOUR MAN

Dear Hubby...

- What are *your* answers to the survey questions in this chapter?

- If I am simply too tired or preoccupied to engage with you in intimacy, does this make you feel that I am rejecting *you*? If so, how can I communicate my inability to you without sending that rejection message?

- Are there things that I am doing for you that are tiring me out but are not, in your mind, as high a priority as this? If so, can you help me understand your priorities, and can we sit down together to develop a plan to either eliminate or find another way to accomplish the other priorities?

- How do you most need to be loved in this area? What can I do to show my cheerful commitment?

- What is your ideal frequency of sex? (Don't gasp at the answer.)

- Here are some needs I'd like to communicate in order for our love life to become more mutually satisfying.

A Quote to Remember:

"Anybody who believes that the way to a man's heart is through his stomach flunked geography." —Robert Byrne

Suggested further reading:

Sheet Music by Kevin Leman

The **BIG** Idea

The one main idea I'm taking away from this week's discussion is:

_____

_____

_____

_____

_____

_____

_____

_____

_____

_____

_____

_____

_____

_____

Chapter 6

KEEPER OF THE VISUAL ROLODEX:

Why It's So Natural for Him to Look and So Hard to Forget What He's Seen

<u>Weekly Challenge Report</u>:

Married women: Did you notice what messages you sent your husband, through your sexual availability or lack of it?

Single women: What messages did you notice the media sending about how men view sex? How does that compare with the findings of *For Women Only*?

The Recap

Even happily married, devoted men are instinctively pulled to look at "eye magnet" women, and most men have a mental Rolodex of stored female images that can intrude upon their thoughts without warning. As upsetting as these truths might be to you, remember that temptation is not sin, and your guy is likely trying his best to minimize those involuntary thoughts and win the battle of the mind. The lure doesn't happen because of you and has nothing to do with his feelings for you; in fact, most men wish they didn't have it. As women, we can be supportive of our men's efforts to keep their thought lives pure, pray for them, champion modesty, and realize God created men to be visual and that His creation is good.

"Images often arise without warning, even if the guy doesn't want them." —Shaunti, FWO, p. 115

"Women who are totally clueless about this problem can also thoughtlessly contribute to it." —Shaunti, FWO, p. 133

Key Questions

1. What challenged you most about this chapter?
2. If it's true that men have a hard time not noticing "eye magnets" and that those images can later intrude upon their thoughts—even if they don't want them to—what is this culture like for our men?
3. What is the difference between temptation and sin?
4. How can we be supportive of men, yet not in any way condone or excuse inappropriate thoughts or actions?

Life Story

After months of financial stress, Blake and Nicole were grateful when Blake began a lucrative two month filming job for a producer of athletic gear, even though it meant he was out of town a lot. The video shoots were at a popular beach resort, and on the phone one night Nicole joked to Blake that she wished she were "slaving away" in that environment too. Blake replied, "Actually, I wish you were here *instead* of me!" When Nicole asked what on earth he meant, he shut down and wouldn't explain. Three weeks into the well-paying job, Nicole was surprised when Blake said he was going to turn the job over to a female colleague. When she asked him why, she was both surprised and dismayed when he confessed that he was having a difficult time being around women with great, athletic bodies in little bikinis all day, and had begun being seriously tempted to turn on inappropriate movies in his hotel room at night. Nicole was devastated that Blake would have either temptation, and she began wondering if she could trust him.

Case Study Questions

1. Can you identify with Nicole's feeling of devastation?

2. In what ways was Blake dishonoring his wife? In what ways was he honoring her?

3. Put yourself in Blake's shoes for a moment. How might he feel about his wife's reaction to his confession? How might he handle such a situation in the future, as a result?

4. How should Nicole handle her feeling of betrayal and the question of whether she can trust Blake?

Guy Perspective: "There's not a day that goes by that I'm not bombarded by the temptation to stare at a beautiful woman. It has nothing to do with my own beautiful wife; it's just like a flashing light that grabs my attention. I'd like to be able to tell my wife when I'm tempted to let the thoughts linger, but I'm afraid it will make her feel insecure."

Gal Response: Does this constant head turning, flashing light problem for men surprise you? Is this something you feel free to discuss with your man? Why or why not?

FWO E-mail Feedback—from a guy: "When I heard your three-part program on *Focus on the Family* recently, I couldn't believe I was hearing my deepest feelings and desires from a strange woman's mouth. As I listened to you and Dr. Dobson talk about men and what makes us tick, I knew I had found a gold mine of information for my wife. And when the second program was over (the one about how a guy is visual and has such a difficult time with noticing other women), I broke down and cried because I knew that's what I had been trying to find a way to tell her for years now. This is our first and will be our only marriage, and of course we try to love each other the only ways we have ever known how. *But* your words and your research gave me the freedom to tell my wife all the struggles I have daily in this sex-saturated culture of America...and I found out I was normal! I explained to her that I do notice other women and how beautiful they are, but it's her face and her body that I think about. Well, you will be happy to know that yesterday I really opened up to her. We had the most intimate and pleasurable experience we have had in years, and we talked until way way past midnight. I got almost no sleep, but today I feel better than I have in a long time. I feel free again. Today, I left work a little early; I wrote her a very personal love letter, bought a single white rose, and took them both and put them in her car.... Things will never be the same with us. Thank you."

Weekly Challenge: As you go about your day, look for images that could be construed as "eye magnets" if you were a man. Make a mental note of what percentage of the women on television or out in public might pose a challenge for a man who wants to honor his wife in his thought life. Evaluate your home environment for ways to help your man in this effort.

BRINGING IT HOME:
DISCUSSING IT WITH YOUR MAN

Dear Hubby...

Author's note: *Because this can be a difficult subject for husbands and wives to discuss, please approach it with discretion and compassion— including skipping the section if your husband prefers not to talk about it. For some couples, it will be better to discuss with the help of a trained counselor.*

- Can you help me understand what it is like when a very attractive woman appears in a man's line of sight?

- About how many times a day do you get bombarded by "eye magnets"? (See pp. 111–112 for explanation.)

- Help me understand how a "mental Rolodex" works? Is there anything that makes images more likely to pop up in your mind, or is it random? How tough is it to erase or replace the images that surface?

- Do you feel free to share your struggles or needs with me in this area?

- How appropriately do you feel I dress? Am I helping or hindering men with my clothing and tone?

- How can I best support you in this area?

A Quote to Remember:

"She looked as if she had been poured into her clothes and had forgotten to say 'when.'" —P. G. Wodehouse

Suggested further reading:

Sex Is Not the Problem (Lust Is) by Joshua Harris

The **BIG** Idea

The one main idea I'm taking away from this week's discussion is:

_____

_____

_____

_____

_____

_____

_____

_____

_____

_____

_____

_____

_____

Chapter 7

CHOCOLATE, FLOWERS, BAIT FISHING

Why the Reluctant Clod You Know Really Does Want Romance

Weekly Challenge Report: Did you notice the difficulties that men might face from the media and the world? Did you take a personal inventory of ways you can support your man in the home environment?

The Recap

Your man really does want romance, but he may feel as though he has poor skills in this area...or he may simply have different ideas about what is romantic. Most men would like more romance—yes, even apart from sex! Our men want connection, fun, and togetherness as much as we do. A guy views taking romantic initiative as a huge risk of humiliation or inadequacy, so you need to encourage him and prove that he's not at risk. Most men also view going out and doing things together as romantic.

"Almost half of these men [surveyed] aren't confident you'll like their romantic efforts." —Shaunti, FWO, p. 141

"Make yourself the kind of friend and lover he constantly wants to pursue." —Shaunti, FWO, p. 153

Key Questions

1. Were you surprised about how men feel about romance?

2. Give an example of when you did something right in encouraging your man's attempts at romance. Give an example when you may have inadvertently shut him down.

3. Consider this quote on p. 150: "'A guy wants romance…to reexperience the spark of dating, to reconnect after days of draining work at the office, to feel love and intimacy, to know he is wanted and enjoyed, and to utterly escape the crushing nonstop pressure of life.'" Do you think the man in your life would agree? Does this change the way you view your responsibility in the area of romantic response?

Life Story

Blake didn't normally cook for the family, but he decided to surprise Nicole on their anniversary by arranging for the kids to stay with a babysitter and making her a romantic dinner. It was beautiful: china, candles, the works. The meal was lasagna, and it looked and smelled terrific. After a few bites, Nicole hopped up and got the salt, pepper, and oregano out of the cupboard. The couple had a nice evening, but in the following weeks Blake didn't respond to Nicole's hints that she'd love another dinner. It wasn't until months later that Blake admitted that he felt like his efforts had been judged to be inadequate that night, and that it would be hard for him to attempt something like that again anytime soon.

Case Study Questions

1. What happened here? Why the hurt feelings from Blake?
2. Put yourself in Blakes's shoes. What might his sensitivity say about any areas of insecurity?
3. What should Nicole have done differently, if anything?

4. Once Blake told her how he felt, how should she respond?

Guy Perspective: "Men are being shredded in the media for not being romantic. We're expected to be inept, and we're made fun of on TV shows like *Everybody Loves Raymond*. It's an uphill battle we're fighting, so we feel we're destined to fail, and expected to fail. We think, 'Why bother if we're going to be laughed at anyway?' But, if we're *not* teased about our feeble attempts—testing the waters of romance with one toe, and if a piranha doesn't come up and bite that toe—it could lead to lots more fun, romantic attempts from us 'unromantic clods.'"

Gal Response: Be honest. Have you ever bitten a toe that was testing the waters of romance?

FWO Female Feedback: "I must say I've been guilty in this area of romance. I think it's because I'm such a control freak that I don't give him the space to make romantic plans. I'm always doing it myself! I have seen that my husband thrives on the praise I give him for his attempts, but then I forget and go back to my old controlling patterns, and he quits trying. Pray for me!"

Weekly Challenge: Try to encourage any romantic moments your man initiates this week. Look for signals that he wants to do something together that he might view as romantic.

BRINGING IT HOME:
DISCUSSING IT WITH YOUR MAN

Dear Hubby...

- What are *your* answers to the survey questions in this chapter?

- When you did this _____, it made me feel like you were doing/saying this: _____. But now I realize maybe you were doing/saying this: _____; is that correct?

- If you view going out and doing things together as romantic, give me some examples of what that might look like.

- What things do I do that encourage or discourage you from pursuing romance with me? If you want romance as I do, what can I do in the future to help?

- In your mind, is romance totally separate from sex? Totally connected? Or is sex unconnected but a nice end to a romantic time together?

A Quote to Remember:

"We've got this gift of love, but love is like a precious plant. You can't just accept it and leave it in the cupboard or just think it's going to get on by itself. You've got to keep watering it; really look after it and nurture it." —John Lennon

Suggested further reading:

The Five Love Languages by Gary Chapman

The **BIG** Idea

The one main idea I'm taking away from this week's discussion is:

_____

_____

_____

_____

_____

_____

_____

_____

_____

_____

_____

_____

Chapter 8

THE TRUTH ABOUT THE WAY YOU LOOK

Why What's on the Outside Matters to Him on the Inside

<u>Weekly Challenge Report</u>: Did you spot any attempts by your man to initiate a romantic "do something together" moment this week?

The Recap

What's on the outside (your appearance) matters to him on the inside. He doesn't need you to be a size 3, but he does want you to make an effort to take care of yourself for him. That makes him feel loved, and helps him make the similarly difficult effort to keep his visual life pure. Men find this subject dangerous and can't honestly express their wishes because they don't want to hurt their wives (which is why this chapter has a different sort of Bringing It Home section). Men don't mind God-given individuality, including sturdy thighs or small boobs, and they even wish their wives weren't so sensitive about their bodies; yet seven out of ten surveyed men said they would be emotionally bothered if their woman let herself go and didn't seem to care about making an effort to improve her appearance. Your man wants to feel proud of you, and he is totally willing to help you.

"We need to accept how complicated and hypersensitive the appearance issue is for both partners." —Shaunti, FWO, p. 159

"The fact that she cares about how she looks is a total turn-on, if you want to know the truth. I tell her all the time how much I appreciate the work she's putting into this." —Man Quote, FWO, p. 165

Key Questions

1. Is the desire of men in this area a legitimate one? Do you believe that if a husband truly loves his wife, then her lack of effort regarding her appearance shouldn't matter to him?

2. Do you think God cares about your appearance? Your energy? Your health?

3. Does this subject make you cringe, anger you, or stir up another strong emotion? If so, why do you think that is the case?

4. Consider the words of the man on p. 169 who says, "Sometimes I'll meet a man whose wife is overweight—but she takes care of herself. She puts some effort into appearance.... If she is comfortable in her

own skin and is confident, you don't notice the extra pounds. I look at that husband and think, *He did well.*'" How does this quote make you feel? How comfortable are you in your skin?

Life Story

After three kids and fifteen years of marriage, Nicole realized she had somehow put on twenty-five extra pounds and along the way had also quit wearing makeup. One day *Blake* joined a gym and started exercising and dieting. He never said a thing, but Nicole noticed that he became pensive if she brought a lot of junk food home from the store. They had a strong marriage, but things just didn't seem as *fun* between them anymore.

Case Study Questions

1. Can you relate?
2. What was Blake trying to communicate?
3. Put yourself in Blake's shoes: *Is* there any way he can productively discuss his feelings with Nicole?
4. What is Nicole's responsibility, if anything?

Guy Perspective: "It's not about becoming an underwear model or having a perfect figure. Appearance is the whole package—friskiness, playfulness, personality, face, voice, touch, posture, and confidence. A smile is the most beautiful thing a woman can put on...better than makeup, more important than great hair. All that being said, however, the effort to look good does really matter. Guys want to be proud of their women. Husbands do want to show off their wives.

"It's really cool and encouraging when you see a little old couple walking along, and she's dressed to the nines and in shape. She's seventy-five or eighty, but her husband is looking at her like she's the most gorgeous thing in town. He's glowing with pride, and his look tells the whole world, "Look at her...This is my baby and you can't have her.

"But if a woman lets herself go, sits in a chair all day and turns into a blob, it is really tough on a guy. Actually, here's a secret: We actually *want* our wives to be attractive to other men...not for them to drag her into a closet, of course. But we feel great when other guys are momentarily drawn into the magnetic charms of our wife...her voice, face, eyes, wit, humor, intelligence, and overall appearance. We like that. It sends a jolt of mild jealousy and pride when we see another man awaken to the beauty that, until that moment, he didn't realize existed in the woman we love."

Gal Response: What do you think about this guy's perspective? Do you think your guy shares this view—that seeing your effort is important? When you look into the mirror, do you see this "whole package" that would bring pride to your man? If not, what steps can you take to incorporate some effort about these appearance-related attributes into the unique tapestry that's you?

FWO Female Feedback: "When I read this chapter, I started weeping. I'm fifty-two years old and never realized that taking care of myself equated to showing my husband how much I loved him. I knew it was time to quit making excuses, get my tail to the gym, and go on a diet. God gave me the grace to do it, and within a year I had lost thirty-five pounds. I can tell you that my husband is now ecstatic. Today he called and said, "Who is that skinny girl I saw in my house this morning?" He's buying me clothes and manicures and really giving me the compliments. I never knew how appreciative he'd be of my efforts. I feel like a new woman, and it's so obvious that he feels loved. I can't thank you enough for giving me this truth in such love."

FWO E-mail Feedback—from a guy: When I read your advice to women about how men really feel about their wife's appearance, it was like a breath of fresh air. I cannot speak with my wife about this topic. I don't want to hurt her feelings, and yet it affects other areas of our relationship in ways that she has not been able to understand. I know that having giving birth to our two-year-old daughter took a toll on her body, and for the first year after that I mentally gave her a lot of slack, figuring that it was just a matter of time before she'd decide she needed to work the pounds off. If she were to ask me about how I feel about her looks right now, I would only be able to truthfully answer, "Honey, I love you no matter what!" But I cannot express to her how unsatisfying it is to make love to her when I feel she is making no effort to lose the pounds and weighs twenty pounds more than I do. Nor can I tell her that when people ask to see a picture of her, I show them one that was taken before she gained all her weight so I can feel proud showing her picture to others. On a fairly regular basis she talks about another diet she wants to try, while on the other hand, with equal regularity continues baking cakes, cookies and brownies and brings home another half gallon of one of her favorite ice cream flavors. I can't say anything because it would be like choosing to swim in shark-infested waters. I do hope that she takes this to heart. It would do so much for our relationship. I am truly glad to know that in the book you emphasized that this is not about a man being shallow, but knowing that our wife loves and cares for us enough to make herself more desirable to us in every way she can.

Weekly Challenge: What are you doing well in your efforts toward appearance? What might be some blind spots?

BRINGING IT HOME:

Unlike the other chapters, we strongly urge you not to talk to your man, but rather, to do the following:

1. Even without looking in the mirror or standing on a scale (as the book made clear, this truth applies to petite, 115-lb women too!), ask yourself if you're really making an honest effort to take care of yourself for your husband.
2. Ask a trusted girlfriend to give you an honest, balanced appraisal, and if necessary, advice on changes you could make. This will also help ensure that you do not spiral out of control over issues that really aren't issues!
3. Pray about all this until you have peace.
4. Then, if necessary, go to your husband with words along these lines:

"Sweetheart, God has convicted me that I have failed to make the effort I used to toward taking care of myself for you, and looking great for you. Will you forgive me? I feel I'm supposed to _____, and I'm asking if you will support me in this by doing _____."

He'll likely be shocked and thrilled, but he may also say something like, "Honey, you know I love you just the way you are." At that point, you do not run to the freezer for some Ben & Jerry's to celebrate your love. You thank him for his unconditional love, and you start your program—including taking him up on his offer of help!

A Quote to Remember:

"Silence is sometimes an answer." —Estonian Proverb

"Sweat plus sacrifice equals success." —Charles O. Finley

Suggested further reading:

Fit for Excellence by Sheri Rose Shepherd

The **BIG** Idea

The one main idea I'm taking away from this week's discussion is:

_____

_____

_____

_____

_____

_____

_____

_____

_____

_____

_____

_____

_____

WORDS FOR
YOUR HEART

What Your Man Most Wishes You Knew About Him

The Recap

There is one thing men wish we knew more than anything else. What surveyed men most wished to convey to women was not how much we could improve our appearance, or which of our attitudes needed adjustment, or how to better our performance in the relationship...but rather, *how much they love us!* (*Sniff...*)

Key Questions

1. Does this surprise you? Why or why not?
2. In what ways might your man be trying to express or show his love that you may not even recognize?
3. How do you respond? How *should* you respond?

4. Consider this final quote on pp. 183–184: "It is so
   true, that behind every great man is a great woman.
   There are a lot of men out there who are mediocre,
   simply because their wives will not support them and
   bring them to greatness. And there are a lot of
   mediocre men who are destined to become great
   men—who are becoming great men—because their
   wives love and support them." How does this state-
   ment make you feel?

5. If you have children, how are you training them now
   to become the kind of husband or wife they'll need
   to be in the future?

Guy Perspective: "Wives don't know how often their husbands will talk about them in glowing terms around other men.
They have no idea. One good friend always says, 'I married way
over my head, and I'm proud of that fact.' Other men can easily
pick up when another guy is head over heels in love with his wife.
Almost all men do, in one way or another, communicate to other
men how great their ladies really are."

Gal Response: Do you think this is true? How do you think
your man talks about you? How would it make you feel to over-
hear "good gossip" about how much your man loves you?

FWO Female Feedback: "I know you said that our goal was
to change *ourselves*, but as I've made some changes based on the

truths in your book, I've seen that my husband is also changing! I now know that he really loves me—deeply and unconditionally, but that he just couldn't express it until I backed off in some areas and made him feel like he could open his heart again, like he did when we first met."

Ongoing Challenge: Are you able, either with your group or alone, to agree to the covenant on the final page of this guide?

BRINGING IT HOME:
DISCUSSING IT WITH YOUR MAN

Dear Hubby...

- Have you ever tried to convey your love for me but ended up feeling like I didn't really believe you?

- Is there anything that I say or do that encourages you in your expressions of love? Discourages you?

- Here is a unique way you make me feel loved:

  _____.

- I want to support you in becoming all God intends you to become. Based on my new understanding of you, what one thing can I commit to do that would most make you feel supported?

A Quote to Remember:

As one well-known pastor told his large congregation: "I know you think you have a good pastor. You don't. You have a *great* pastor's wife."

Suggested further reading:

Communication: Key to Your Marriage by H. Norman Wright

The Big Idea

The one main idea I'm taking away from this week's discussion is:

_____

_____

_____

_____

_____

_____

_____

_____

_____

_____

_____

_____

_____

APPENDIX:

A. How Two Very Different Groups Used This Guide

We have found that the women who use this discussion guide are from all walks of life and all stages of spiritual development, and in all different size groups: from three women in a coffee shop, to five hundred in a large church auditorium. We thought it would be helpful for group facilitators to see how two very different types of discussion groups actually organized their meetings and used the mix-and-match elements of this Guide.

1. Large Group/Church Setting

At Calvary Community Church in Sumner, Washington, the ladies use this discussion guide in their upbeat, large weekly meetings. The following is an interview with Mary Armstrong, the pastor's wife and head of Women's Ministries, and the specific information she provided about their group process.

"We're using the *For Women Only* book and discussion guide in a large seven-week study group with 250 women. We're creating a fun, small-group-oriented focus in a large setting, with the women sitting at round tables in a large auditorium. The facilitator at each table starts with the Weekly Challenge, and then we move through each section of the discussion guide, adding a couple of our own elements to each session."

Here's the order of events at Calvary, which takes about two hours on a weeknight:

1. Mingling/Coffee. (15 minutes)
2. Weekly Challenge, which is flashed up on the large screen through PowerPoint, and informal discussion at tables. (15 minutes)
3. Welcome/IceBreaker—Begins with silliness like doing the Macarena. (10 minutes)
4. Worship. (10 minutes)
5. Recap and Key Questions in small groups at tables. (30 minutes)
6. A movie video clip that illustrates the point. For instance, this week's was pulled from *How to Lose a Guy in 10 Days*. (2 minutes)
7. True Life Story—the church's drama team actually re-creates the case study as a short drama skit, so everyone can see it played out. Sometimes they show an additional cartoon on the big screen. (10 minutes)
8. Story and Drama Discussion in small groups, asking what the couple did wrong, and what they did right, using some of the specific questions in the Guide. (5 minutes)
9. Guy Perspective, also up on PowerPoint. Short comment on that. (2 minutes)
10. "Guy Perspective" talk from a man in the church on that specific subject. (Yes, they let one man in

the building during the course of the evening!)
(10 minutes)

11. God's Perspective—Looking deeper into what the Bible says about each topic, investigated ahead of time by one of the facilitators and shared with the other small group leaders prior to the evening's discussion. (20 minutes) Sometimes they have give-aways after this time, such as Band-Aids to remind us to close our mouths, a measuring tape to remember the measure of a man, etc.

The leaders and facilitators also meet thirty minutes prior to the assembly to debrief from the prior week, go over any challenges, and come up to speed on the Bible verses that will be used in the final section.

Mary advises facilitators to make it *fun!* "These topics can be heavy, and there are lots of hurting women out there—single, married, divorced, and separated. Life is hard, so make it fun and entertaining. Allow the Lord to minister to the women, but include lots of upbeat music, bright graphics, and humor in the skits."

2. Small Group Setting

A little coffee group in Atlanta, Georgia, did things quite differently. Here's what was shared by Rose Caudill, who started the small group:

"It's great to start meeting at a coffee house, but as the group gets larger, and as more women begin opening up about the tough issues in the book, it's a good idea to move to private homes. We sent out an e-mail inviting women to attend, and we told them to come as they were…that we weren't concerned with carpet stains or fixing elaborate food…that it was just a time to relax and get real with friends."

Rose and her group have had fun with subject matter. She cautions, however, that someone needs to be the clear lead teacher, or facilitator, or the group may flounder and get way off track. They had to rein things in several times in the beginning.

This small group does not use the discussion guide in a formal, step-by-step process, but rather, they choose the one or two sections that most need discussion and reflection that week.

As the weeks have progressed, the women have become more open and vulnerable, even sharing very personal things about their lives. That's why Rose cautions the women, "What's shared in the group stays in the group." It's important for the women to be confident that the other women will be safe with their hearts.

The greatest thing about using the guide, Rose believes, is that it lets women know they're not alone in their struggles, and that their marriage challenges are normal! "So many women think they're alone, but as we read the book and discussion guide, we're seeing that we're not. It's been such an encouragement."

Now that my eyes have been opened to my man's inner life, I will...

1. Assume the best about him as a man made in God's image, and do my part to understand his unique desires and needs.
2. Choose to trust him and join the adventure, even when he's driving in circles and won't ask for directions.
3. Catch myself before I complain about him to others, and brag on him instead.
4. Every day, find something he's really good at, and then affirm him in that area.
5. Notice how he feels about providing, and thank him for his commitment.
6. Recognize that my husband doesn't just want more sex; he also needs to feel that I *desire* and *enjoy* him sexually.
7. Pray daily for him in our visually distracting culture, and support and appreciate his efforts to keep his thought life pure.
8. Understand that he may be proposing a romantic rendezvous when he says, "Hey, honey—wanna go to Home Depot with me?"
9. Make sure he knows I take my appearance seriously, and that he sees me making an effort to take care of myself for him.
10. Embrace his efforts to tell me how much he loves me— in whatever way he conveys that best—and let him know that I believe him.

Printed in the United States
by Baker & Taylor Publisher Services